Work To Invest

Jason Ballay

Return to Project Home

DEDICATION

I dedicate this book to my father who I lost at a young age of 11. His death made me grow up faster than the regular kid and all the hard working families living paycheck to paycheck, trying to make a better living for their families, just like how my mom did. I also want to specially dedicate this book to my mother for working so hard to provide for us even when times were tough and for believing in me. Also to my wife for staying focused on our goals and following our dreams.

WORK TO INVEST

Let your investments pay your
bills, create financial freedom

JASON BALLAY

CONTENTS

ACKNOWLEDGMENTS

Friends, Family, Coworkers, Clients, and my students.

Work to Invest not Work to pay bills - Create multiple streams of income, let your investments pay your bills.

Written by Jason Ballay

Always have an investment plan in your life. People would ask me why I invest in rentals, businesses and dividend stocks. Well, you never know what will happen to your job, a stream of income or your life. An investment plan or plan B is important because social security might not be there by the time you retire and from the looks of things, it will not be there.

You need to invest like you are about to lose your job, invest as much as you can afford, don't work to pay bills, work to invest like the title goes. I think the reason why a lot of people don't invest is because they don't see the results right away, and they want it instantly. Most people don't want to wait to see the benefits from investing when they retire. Well, I hope this book can change your way of thinking about investing and how to see money.

Tip:
An investment plan is an insurance on your income, your salary. You have insurance on your car why not on your income.

1ˢᵀ CHAPTER
INTRODUCTION

Bio, Examples & the Beginning

Please allow me to introduce myself... my name is Jason Ballay.

Since 2004 I have been investing and in 2014, I had financial freedom (the point where my income equaled the same as my job salary) and each year, my income increases more and more because I reinvest my earnings. I created this book because people ask me all the time "what should I invest in" and I will ask them how much do you know about investments, and sometimes they would say I know a few things or they will say "not much". Also, I will ask them "what's for sale?" Is real estate cheap, what stocks are undervalued or what stocks are paying great dividends? Do they have a business for sale because the owner is retiring and doesn't want the business anymore? When I ask people these questions, their eyes would light up all big and they would say "you know what, you are right." You have to invest in the things that have great deals. It is one of the best feelings to have when you are working to invest in your portfolio of investments (real estate, stocks, and businesses) and not to work because you need to pay bills and make ends meet. Living pay check to pay check is not the best way to live.

I remember being at work on a Thursday and I walked to the front desk and saw about 10 of my coworkers waiting. I asked the clerk behind the desk "what is everyone waiting for?" And the clerk said, "It's Thursday and they are waiting for their paychecks and the checks are late." I saw one of my coworkers and I asked him "why are you here on your day off," he said "I have to get my check," I asked him "why don't you get it on Friday when you come back to work?" He said, "I can't because I need to pay rent, the light and water bill." This way of living is very hard on a family. Another reason I created this book is because I was tired of seeing my coworkers, vendors, brokers and friends lose their jobs and they had nothing to fall back on. Nothing that would pay any bills and help out with other payments. Well, I know what you must be thinking now… Jason, they have a severance package that would sustain them till they find something else. I only know of two people that received such a package vs over 20 workers that lost their job and had nothing other than some life savings of less than 6 months, 401K saved up or some vacation time that was left over. Also one of the persons that received a severance package is still working because it's not enough to live off of and he wanted something else to do rather than stay at home since he was about to retire.

While I was working as a distributor, I saw my sales reps and co-workers losing their jobs due to cutbacks and reorganizations. One sales rep for a manufacturing department survived four cut backs (aka reorganization). They eventually fired all the company's sales reps and decided to use brokers to represent their products. Even at the company, I worked for, while I was in a meeting with my boss and we were talking about a few things he said something that amazed me, "everyone is replaceable, even me and even the president of the company." He was right, everyone has a replacement, no matter how much they bring to the table or even how much they know and are able to do. Everyone is replaceable! That's why it's important to keep investing in yourself. Another example is my neighbor who had a similar situation. One day I saw my neighbor outside and I looked to the left and I noticed a "For Sale" sign in his front yard, I asked him what happened, I thought you loved this house? He said, "I do, but I lost my job with the company I have been working with for over 20 years and what sucks more is that I trained my replacement. I asked my boss after a few weeks and said: "the person I am training, am I getting promoted or am I being fired?" My boss replied, "he is your replacement and we are letting you go, we are downsizing" without missing a beat. I was shocked when my neighbor told me this and I asked him if he had another job or something lined up and he said, "no I wish I did, I wish I had something to fall back on. I'm just going back home to be with my old friends and relatives and hopefully, I might find something."

So I told him "I can ask around for you to see if anybody is looking for someone and if you need anything like advice or help, here is my info" and he said, "thank you I will keep in touch." He looked down and said "I wish I did things differently, like investing or partnering with my friend to create a business. We would have created an engineering firm, but I didn't think I would get fired. So I am going to move and just be with my family." I never heard from him again but I realize that we always need a backup plan or something to fall back on, something to help pay our bills. So I always made sure I lived below my means and invest as if I'm about to lose my job. It may actually happen any day, you never know what could happen. I can make a mistake that would cost 10's of thousands of dollars by just forgetting a few easy steps. So I knew I needed something just in case I was let go or when I am ready to leave I would have some income coming in.

Tip:
Make sure your resume is updated every year or every two years. It's easier to keep up with it if something happens.

2ND CHAPTER
FOUNDATION

Not having an investment plan is like having no car insurance on your favorite car. Think of your investment plan as insurance on your income or on your job. I know some people that have insurance on everything but not on the most important thing which is their income. They just want to pay the bills but they didn't have any insurance on their income.

I am going to explain some of the ways you can create extra income and protect your income. It will definitely make paying those unexpected bills that pop up like car repairs, house repairs, time for a new car, easier to pay off and so that you will not drown in debt.

I hear so many people say, I will only put away 10% of my income into a 401k and that should be enough for my retirement, but I encourage you to invest like you are about to lose your job, invest like you are not going to have an income tomorrow. You need to save every penny and reinvest it. Why wait till you retire to enjoy the hard work of your savings while making others rich. Invest as much as you can now. I will explain the ways to do it and some things to invest into that will create multiple streams of income. Trust me it's the best feeling in the world when you realize that you are working hard to invest instead of killing yourself to pay bills and make ends meet.

To be wealthy or to even double your income, you need to change the way you look at money going forward and how you see the world. It might not happen right away but you will start looking at your environment differently. Let's say you are driving down the street and you see cars with their business logo on it or an 18 wheeler hauling freight on it. Instead of seeing a car with a logo or 18 wheeler, you should see a company generating money or an 18 wheeler, shipping products to make money for the company and helping the gas station make a profit by buying fuel. The driver is also making money by delivering the goods.

Let's try something out, close your eyes (if you are reading this book, you would have to read it first before closing your eyes lol.) Close your eyes and picture yourself on the corner of a busy street. You look around and see buildings, cafe, stores, cars, people shopping, and you look up and you see streams of dollar bills in the air going in multiple directions. One stream of money is tenants paying rent, another stream is people buying coffee at the cafe, streams of money for expenses like utilities, phone, cable, insurance. Even the government has streams of money, property taxes, sales tax, and meter payments. Now the key here is to find a way to direct these streams of income to you. How can you be a landlord in order to get that monthly rent? How can you be that business owner to receive the money from the sale of coffee? With these examples, you will start to see the world differently and you will increase your income and become wealthy.

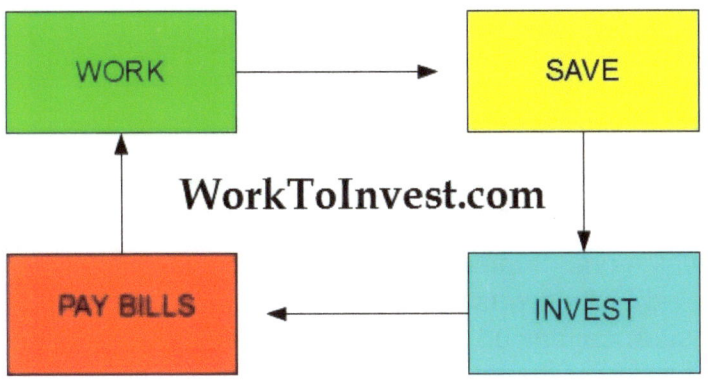

Expenses:

It's very important to control your expense either by getting rid of that expense or reducing that expense. Let's take a look at the list of all your expenses. Even to monitor your monthly credit score for your average grocery bill, gasoline, electric bill, cell phone, so that a credit card company can alert you about credit is $3.99. Remove this $3.99 expense you are wasting money. A lot of these companies don't do anything special. Take a look at your credit card bill or bank statement to have an idea of your expenses.

Electric Bill (Avg)   Water Bill (Avg)
Natural Gas   Cable/Satellite
Cell Phone   House Phone
Car Maintenance   Gasoline

Car Insurance	Car Note
Food/Grocery	Going out to eat (lunch, dinner)
Gym Membership	Rent/Mortgage
Credit card interest	Stamps
Expense 1	Expense 2
Expense 3	*Expense 4*

Which one of these items listed above can be reduced or canceled? When was the last time you shopped around for car insurance, call up or go online to check what their rates are? Talking of insurance, when was the last time you priced your insurance on your house or even your car insurance? This is a huge expense that always gets overlooked because people don't think about it since the policy is in their escrow account or they don't want to bother about it. Can you cancel a miscellaneous expense like credit lock, Netflix, Cable, Pandora or Sirius to save money per month? Take an expense and ask yourself; can this expense be canceled or can I reduce this expense? Like your cable bill, a lot of people have every movie package you can think of. They also go online and watch TV thru the net.

Now remember the key to cutting these expenses is to invest these savings into investment plans, don't take these savings and start spending your money on crazy things that are not needed. The same goes with a new job that pays more money. Don't just think that because you make more money, you can afford it now. No, if you start to make more money, invest your new salary into something that makes more money. If you get a 5% raise or find a new job that pays more, you need to change your way of thinking and say; okay I am getting paid more so I can invest more. A lot of people like to put their money in the bank and keep it there but that is a bad idea because your money should be working hard to make you more money. Think of it as a game of hot potato, you have to know where to put your money and that is an investment.

This book is broken up into three main sections:

1. Dividend Stocks
2. Real Estate
3. Business

Let's take a look at different vehicles that can pay for your expense.

3RD CHAPTER
DIVIDEND

Investment Plan Section: Dividend Stocks

How did I get into dividend investing? I heard the word "REIT" on a morning radio talk show on my way to work and the person that was talking kept saying "this business is a REIT of Real Estate." I did a search on my phone for this term to see what it was all about and since I like real estate and I had rental properties, it caught my attention. REIT stands for (Real Estate Investment Trust) and I bought a book that explains how a REIT and other Dividend-paying stocks like MLP (Master Limited Partnerships) works. REIT is an easy way to buy an interest in Commercial Properties like apartment buildings, malls, retail buildings, storage units, restaurant buildings, retirement homes and health care buildings. MLP stands for (Master Limited Partnerships) and these companies invest in oil and natural gas related industries like oil fields, pipelines, processing plants and tankers. They are actually getting into gasoline related sales lately, but be careful, a lot of these companies are affected by oil prices. If oil price drops too much, these companies will shut down till prices are back up. When this happens, production will go down and so does profit and then the stock price drops which will also cause dividend payments to drop. Just remember to hang in there and don't run to the hills to sell everything. The price already fell and if you sell, then you lost anyway. Just ride out the market, if possible when the price drops, that is the best time to buy, so try to buy before the price increases.

REIT and MLP companies usually pay out 80% of their profit as dividends by law because they are not double taxed like a regular corporation and invest in big name dividend paying companies.

Tip:
MLP's are linked to oil prices, if the price of oil goes down then they can't produce. When there is no production, then the value of the stock goes down.

Have a mixed portfolio of monthly stocks and quarterly stocks. Have both REIT, MLP stocks and other big name (blue chips) companies paying dividends like AT&T, Verizon, 3M, Altria, and so many more stocks that pay out dividends. For more info go to www.dividend.com

401K & IRAs

Here is my suggestion, stay away from mutual funds, 401K, IRAs and those other so-called retirement funds. The rich don't invest in mutual funds because the returns are too low. I learned this recently while learning more about the stock market and dividend stocks. Mutual funds pay out fees that you are not aware of, they pay out the fund holder, they pay the financial adviser, and on top of that, after these people received their money from the money you invested in certain funds, they charge you a fee every quarter to print out papers and other miscellaneous fees. Now this explains why my money never grew and took forever to come back to where it was before the mortgage crises. After learning this, I just closed out my account and told my financial adviser to mail me a check, after they charged me a processing fee of course. I took this money and invested a portion in real estate and I also invested the rest in Dividend Stocks. Now the money from my closed 401K account is working hard for me. Another thing I don't like about mutual funds is that you don't know all the companies they invest in and what kinds of companies. Yes, they will give you general terms like "International Funds," "Low-Risk Funds," "High-Risk Funds," "Retirement 65" and so on. The only people making fat paychecks are the fund managers and almost all of these guys are just playing a guessing game with your money anyway.

Like they say, if you want something done right then do it yourself. So you might as well find those 20 to 30 companies to invest in and grow your investment plan on your own. You have to ask your coworkers about the 401K and get an idea of how it is performing and the contributions that the company gives to the plan. I worked for one company and every couple of years they would deposit a portion of the company's profits to the 401K plan. Find out if your company does this and if it is something you need to explore because the company I worked for deposited an average of $2,500 to $3K on top of the regular contributions. If this is not the case then make the decision to do both or just do investments like real estate and stocks. I know so many people that have a 401K and when they quit a job or get fired, they forget to take care of the 401K to transfer it.

Rather than invest the money, they feel that this money can help to buy things like a down payment for a car, furniture, riding lawn mower and the list goes on. Now you have to pay a fee and taxes on this money which makes it wrong to use your 401K. You need to have a plan in the beginning and a process before you get a lump sum of money like a 401K or an insurance claim check. When you have a plan, you will know what to do with this money right away.

The Story about 401K

I know you can relate to this story or you may know someone that can relate to it. My mom worked on her retirement 401K for over 20 years and she hit the age where she couldn't work anymore because of health reasons. So she lived off her savings for so many years and one day she needed some money to update the house. She talked to her financial advisers and said to him "I am ready to make my withdrawal" and the financial adviser told my mom "sorry Ms. but you can't because you didn't reach the correct retirement age of your policy and you will have to pay a heavy fee and a tax, on that money if you make a withdrawal. You will lose so much money." So my mother only had a few more years left to hit the proper age. A few years passed and then 9/11 happened, she lost over $20K in savings and this is small in comparison to a lot of people. Some lost $80K to $100K in their 401K retirement.

I remember like it was yesterday, she was crying so much. I asked her what happen, she said "read this letter from the mutual fund company. I lost thousands of dollars and I wanted to take this money out years ago and the market manager told me not to because I would get charged a penalty fee and I will have to pay taxes." I felt so sad for my mom, she worked so hard to do the right thing just like so many other people. Once again my mom called up the financial adviser and said "I want my money and I want it now," plus many other words that would make your jaw drop. Once again, the financial adviser told her, "I know you are upset with the loss but if you withdraw the funds now then you will lose and you need to wait till the market comes back so the price will rise. To make up for the loss just give it some time. She waited years for it to come back and she only gained a few thousand back into her account. So after many years, I recommended my mom to transfer the funds to an IRA which was very diverse and was managed by one of my friends who can recommend a great plan for her. So everything went well for a few years and guess what, the crash happened next? The housing crash happened next but this time, she only lost about $8K.

Once again she had to go through all this again crying, praying and asking why this is happening to her. I felt so bad because I made the recommendation for her but she wasn't mad at me. She knew I tried to help but her ex-coworker lost way more and she has been with the same funds manager ever since the ex-coworker left the company. After these two crashes, she was done with 401K and IRAs and told her financial planner "please close my account, I'm done with this fraud of a system. I lost more money than I made, this is a scam."
Her story is part of the reason why I created this book to show people how to have a diverse investment plan so they don't have to suffer the loss that my mom experienced.

A long time ago, investing in stocks meant that you were investing for a piece of the profits called a dividend but over time, this mindset has changed. Now, investing in stocks is all about, I hope the stock goes up so I can hurry up and sell the stock ASAP. I feel that this style of investing is a lose-lose situation and you can't predict which stocks will go up. There are so many factors that come to play and if this is the case, you will have your money sitting in a company for years waiting for the price to go up and hopefully this company pays out a dividend since your money is tied up.

One of the good things about having a dividend portfolio is that it shows assets and reserves and banks like to see reserves usually around 3 to 6 months worth of expenses. By investing in dividend stocks, you can get a small piece of the action right away, unlike real estate you need to have 20% to 25% down payment to get a rental property and a few other things like reserves and a credit score above 650

Just as real estate is risky, dividend stocks are risky as well. Stock prices could fall, there could be an increase in the interest rates, and/or changes in government laws. The

CEO or president of the company could retire or can be replaced, OPEC could control the price of oil, there could be inflation, however, the markets goes down and then goes back up just like a roller coaster.

Tip:
Just like in life, you have to be diverse just like your stock dividends.

Invest in the long term, don't look at the price of the stock every day and at every chance you get. Once you buy the stock, it's yours. Remember that you bought the stock for the dividend payment not because the price will be going up every day. This is a different type of investment. If the price goes down, it's probably because investors sold because they got scared or just moved on to buy something else. Think of it like this, when you buy a house, don't you order for an appraisal to see how much your house is worth every month? So don't look at the price of the stock every day and every week, just check out the price every 3 months or so. I know it's hard in the beginning but you will get used to it and your portfolio will grow. The value will increase and when the market is down, don't just hurry up and sell, try to ride it out. Evaluate the market and if the price is going down, think of it as stocks going on sale and time to buy more.

A question that I get sometimes is when should I sell my stocks? Don't sell unless you have to and consider selling when the price of the stock is greater than 5 to 6 years worth of dividend payments, and no less. For example, let's say you have 100 shares of XYZ company that pays a monthly dividend of $0.202 per share (100 x .202 = $20.20 dividend payment) bought at $25 a share and over a period of time, the price of that share is $40 dollars so now the value of that stock is worth $1,500 ($40 - $25 = $15 x 100 = $1,500). The dividend payment of over 5 years is $1,212 (60 months x $20.20). Which means that it will take you over 5 years to make the money spent on the payments of this stock and to be the same as the value of the stock ($1500 vs $1,212).

With this example, the price of the stock is greater than the monthly dividend stock, so if you think you want to sell it, then it's okay to sell if you choose to. But if you sell the stocks, remember to reinvest that money into something else like real estate or another stock. Don't go on a shopping spree with this money.

One of the hardest things that people have a hard time changing is their way of thinking when the price of stock fall. Think of it like this, do you buy more steaks when they are on sale or when the price is high because there is a short supply of beef? You can also think of it like this; when the price of gas is high, do you buy a full tank or just what you need and when the price is cheap you buy a full tank of gas. Stocks are the same way. Remember once you buy the stock and the price falls, just don't abandon ship and sell right away. The reason why you bought this stock was because of the dividend payment. When the price of the stock falls, buy more of it. Warren Buffet once said he hates when the price of stocks go up because now he has to pay more for the same stock. Warren likes it when the price goes down because now he can buy more stocks on discount. Over time, you will learn how to determine what price is a good price for a stock and what price is a very low price for a stock and is a bargain. Just like real estate, you will learn what price is a great deal on a property.

One of your goals is to have 1000 shares of stock per company mixed between 10 and 20 companies or more if you find more companies that you like and have an interest in. If you can do this, you will start to see the real power of investing in dividend stocks. Once you are done with 1000 shares, then the next step is to get to 2000 shares of different companies and be diverse because being diverse is the key. Don't try to do this all once and just buy 1000 shares of company one and buy 1000 shares of company two. What I like to do is take $2000, find a company that I want to invest in and buy $2000 worth of shares and find the next company that I am interested in that meets my criteria and buy $2000 shares of that company. This trick works for me, it makes it easier for me to invest, saves time, and helps me to be more of a disciplined investor. You have to determine if this is something you would like to do. My bank sent me a letter in the mail offering a line of credit to do whatever you want to do, remodel the kitchen or take a vacation. However, I wanted to use this line of credit for investing. So I sat down with the bank officer and I showed her the letter I received in the mail.

She asked me "how much credit do I need I ask for the max," so I said $20,000. Her eyes lit up and she said well, let's see what we can do after paperwork and she had to make two phone calls and came back with $12,000 offer. So in reality, that is $2,000 more than I expected. Keep in mind that they charge interest on the balance so watch your expense on this. Now I used this line of credit and started investing, I don't use this line of credit for anything else. One day I walked into a major bank to close out a checking account because I didn't need it anymore for a business I was no longer running. I closed out the account and the bank officer told me they were having an offer on a line of credit, good as cash with 0% interest for 12 months but I only had three months to use it and they charged processing fee 2% of the loan amount. I told the bank officer not a problem, I know exactly what to use it for and smiled. Can you guess what I used the loan for? You guessed right, I reinvested the funds into stocks and I made a couple of extra payments on a rental property loan to get the principle down so I can pay off the mortgage faster. But you see I didn't use the money to buy gifts, presents, or a fancy vacation, think of this loan as good debt because now this money will work for me every month. When money comes your way, you have to use it wisely.

The companies are real but I want to keep them confidential so you can invest in the companies you like and not the one that someone else does, but this gives you an idea of what I am talking about:

1000 shares of REIT = XYZ @ 0.19 = $190 per month 4.8% Yield

1000 shares of MLP = ZXY @ 0.104 = $104 per month 12.43% Yield

1000 shares of REIT = ABC @ 0.125 = $125 per month 9.72% Yield

1000 shares of MLP = CBA @ 0.182 = $182 per month 10.84% Yield

This is $601 per month from only 4 companies, do this for 10 to 20 companies and if you don't have a lifestyle change and a different view on investing, then maybe when you get to 2,000 shares you will do something. I wish my economics teacher in 10th grade that taught me this part of stocks of dividend payments, we only learned about the price of a stock and how to look it up in the newspaper. Do a comparison with your 401K or IRA to these figures, are you getting this kind of returns?

Tip:
You need to learn the rule of 72, this is the rule of how long would it take to double your money, it's pretty easy to learn, take 72 and divide by the rate of return. That equals to how long it will take to double your money, for example, 6% return on your money. (72/6 = 12 years) let's look at another like 1.25% (72 / 1.25 = 57.6)

Check out this website for more information on how to find great stocks paying dividends www.Dividend.com for more investing. Most of your big corporations pay their dividends on a quarterly basis like AT&T, Verizon, Altria, General Mills, and Proctor Gamble.

Tip:

Once you invest in a stock, you will get letters in the mail about the company and votes. So make sure when you set up your brokerage account, that you use your PO Box for this stuff. Your dividend payments will go into your brokerage account and you can withdraw it like a checking account.

Second Heads Up: You will also start getting emails about the latest and greatest stocks from awesome new companies with great new ideas and great products asking you to sign up to a newsletter or program. Just be very cautious about this information and stay on track. Don't get caught up in the marketing programs, they will try to sell you a membership or a video that will show you these special companies to invest in, so be careful.

**Dividend
Helpful Websites**
www.Dividend.com
www.DividendInvestor.com
www.Scottrade.com
www.Etrade.com

Books I found to be helpful

"Investing in REITS" by Ralph L. Block
"Millionaire Teacher" by Andrew Hallam

4TH CHAPTER
REAL ESTATE

Investment Plan Section: Real Estate

What caught my attention with Real Estate? I was at work and my coworker was sitting on the bench. We were talking about houses, places to live, neighborhoods, and that was when he told me that I could buy a triplex, live in one unit and rent out the others and I asked him "what do you mean?" He took out a sheet of paper and drew a picture for me, three squares (triplex rental) and a stick figure (me) living in one unit and then he drew two lines saying; every month they will pay you rent. Then I asked him, wouldn't that cause issues if you live that close to the tenants and they will be your friend and not want to pay you? He said not at all. Although you are the owner, you don't even have to tell them you are the owner. Just tell them you are the manager and get the rules out the way and lay down the policy. Then I asked how can I afford a building of three or four units? He looked at me, shrugged his shoulders and then pointed to me and said you will figure it out, trust me. If you want something bad enough you will find a way to get it. That night, my mind was going 100 mph and I was thinking about the situation, thinking about owning more than one building and getting money from multiple units per month. That night I started doing research, buying books, asking friends and started writing notes. When I started learning more about rentals, the pros, and cons, I was turned off by it. Because I found it slow, more work and little money. I stopped learning and stopped pursuing the matter. A couple of years later, I started looking into it again and then I realized that I was forgetting about the long term goal and the opportunities that it would open up. I also realized that you have to buy the property at the right price, even if you have to fix it up. I discovered that the numbers do work and that was the missing piece that I didn't see. You have to buy it right under value in the beginning after some years, then you can put a large lump sum on a rental building of 3, 4, 5 units.

Treat rental properties like a business from the very beginning and invest and work your rentals for the long term. Example: buy replacement parts that are going to last the longest and what is going to look the best for the next tenant. Don't buy cheap replacement parts. Stay ahead of vacancies and when tenants are about to move out. It's like you are always preparing for the next vacancy and the next new tenant.

Start working on your credit score as early as you can, make sure you have three lines of credit minimum. You need about 5 credit cards but start working on 3 credit cards, use one credit card to pay for something simple like a cell phone bill and a utility bill if they accept credit cards. The 2nd credit card can be used for your cable bill or internet bill and then lock up these two credit cards away and don't use them for anything else. Use the 3rd credit card to pay for gasoline, and other vehicle expenses only and that's it, nothing else. Later on, you can just open the 4th and 5th credit card or department card for your favorite stores like Sears, Dillard's, Lowes, Target, or other department stores that you shop at, but don't use them. I use my Home Depot card only when I have a large purchase because they offer 0% finance for 6 months.

Important: When you pay off your line of credit like a car, note your credit score starts to drop because the line of credit is paid off and you don't have to make any more payments so you are not getting any more credit of payment history when the loan is paid off.

Reminder: Time heals all when it comes to credit repair.

Here is a link to help with tips and any other advice that is added.
Click here for credit score tips - JasonBallay.com

Start using a professional tax person at a place that does bookkeeping and taxes year round. In the beginning, all you will need is someone to help you with your tax filings and to do your taxes so you can start claiming expenses, interest, and depreciation. Stay away from national franchise tax services, they are overpriced and have a high turnover rate. Also just because you have a person to do your taxes doesn't mean you don't need to learn about taxes. I advise you to learn about taxes as well the laws and rules. Once you know what to claim, start keeping an excel file of all expenses and write on the receipt what property this was used for. One of the things that helped me was, I downloaded one of the forms that deal with real estate and looked at the deduction that you can claim as an expense on a property like insurance, repairs, property taxes, mortgage interest, and so much more. Go to IRS.gov and look for "schedule e" - (supplemental income and loss) and take a look at your last year's tax filings and really go over the information. Too many people just take the papers and throw them in the car until they get destroyed or ruined. When dealing with banks, always try to get a PDF copy sent to you or maybe saved on a jump drive. Trust me this will save you time when they ask for a copy of your tax returns for two years ago.

Because foreclosures, bank owned properties, HUD Houses, and a few others are so cheap, don't be shocked that a real estate agent might not work that hard for you. You will be doing a lot of searching and going to neighborhoods to see if they are good. It's because real estate agents don't make that much money from these type of houses because they are cheap. Realtors don't like to deal with them, if they get just their regular commission, they won't make any money. Banks had to come back and offer these agents more money so they can sell them to the public. So don't be shocked if you are doing all the looking and ask an agent to show you a house and next thing you know you don't get a phone call back. Sometimes you are better off just calling the agent that has the listing and ask for a convenient time for you to see the house, except you find a good realtor or maybe a realtor's assistant that is willing to work with you.

The best time to get a line of credit is when you don't need it, so when the chance comes up, get the line of credit from your local bank and try other banks in the area and online. Try Banks like Wells Fargo, Bank of America, it does not hurt to try. I didn't need the money per say, but I knew that one day I would need it for whatever reason. So I checked with my local bank, they had a program for a line of credit to do whatever you need; remodel, car purchase, vacation, or whatever you need it for. I talked to the bank loan specialist and they said I qualified, how much are you interested in doing, always go for the max. I said $25,000 after some phone calls, I was approved for $15,000 line of credit which was better than I thought because I was thinking I could only get $10K. So this worked out great and then I repeated the process with a second bank and they approved $10,000. Even my credit card offered me a line of credit cash up to $6,000 and every once in a while they will have a special 0% for 12 months or 6 months. Now keep in mind, only use these lines of credit to purchase assets and nothing else.

Use your line of credit to help pay down your mortgage on your rental property. Use your line of credit to grow your business, to buy equipment or just use your line of credit to help buy your next rental property. You can also use your line of credit to buy Dividend Stocks, just remember when doing this, you should look at your fees vs your returns when using your L.O.C. on buying Dividend Stocks. Don't use your line of credit to go shopping or to pay for a vacation, let your investments pay for your vacation. Use your line of credit to build your assets only. A line of credit is a **powerful tool** for building wealth so use it wisely. Later on, once you have enough properties and if one of your properties is paid off, you can get a line of credit of around 60% of the equity of the property. Now this is a powerful tool, and you can easily use it to grow your investment properties.

Very Important – put your PO Box on your checks, when at the bank, make sure this is told to the banker that you want your PO box on your checks, so start putting your checks on everything. This will help keep your address secret when returning deposits to tenants. So start using your PO Box whenever possible. Also set up a separate email address for real estate, don't use your personal email address for real estate, it's best to keep it separate. If you have a Gmail account, you can get a Google voice mail box and you can forward this number to any phone, great idea if you have to travel or go out of town. This is good to have because you will get many emails and phone calls about the property listed and even if you have any other properties available.

Tip:
Change your mailing address for your credit cards to your PO Box and from now on you can use your PO Box as the zip code instead of the city you live in at the gas station pump when it asks you for your zip code. In my area, the zip codes for the PO Box is different from the zip codes from my city. This is a little-added security feature so someone can't guess your city zip code on your credit card.

Buy a notebook, break it up into three parts: notes from real estate books/notes from your Dividends/websites with passwords & id's / and other information.
Also, buy a binder that is separated by the alphabets for lease agreements and applications, keep the original copies

When submitting bids on houses always negotiate, for this is the best part and if not try to make it fun and interesting. Never go in with your best price, they will always counter your offer. Always go in below your best price and stay below that price even if they counter again. I was told by a bank that they always have to counter your offer and ask for more because the bank investors will say you didn't try, you didn't even ask for more. But if they ask for more and you counter, the underwriter will see that they tried to go for more. Also if there is something you like on the property, make sure it's in the contract. Later on after a few deals you will get better and start asking for more things to sweeten the pot – remember you are the one with the money.

Yes, with rental properties one month you might work on something simple like fixing a door knob and the next month you need to get someone to fix an A/c unit. Some months you make easy money and not have to do nothing that month. Some months you have to work for the money and some months you don't have to anything except pick up the checks from the PO Box and bring the checks to the bank. This will save you a lot of time and problems down the road. When you have a new tenant, explain to them if something needs repair to let you know and you will send them a number to call to set up an appointment for the repair man so someone can be there. I have the phone number to my repairman in the lease so they know right away on who to call and set up an appointment. On my side, I let the repairman know via text message with the address and phone number of the tenant. After a while, they will have their phone numbers saved and they will know each other on a first name basis. After the repair is completed, pay your repair techs right away, don't waste their time by saying tomorrow or next week, especially if they do the repair right away. Also after some trial and error, you will have an idea of what repairs will cost and what is modest and what is high.

Tip:
Sign up for a Google voice phone number it's a nice feature and it's free.

If you have a mortgage try to pay off the balance within 10 years or less if not no more than 15 years. Try not to go over because when you have paid all that interest, a cheap house of $65 thousand will now be around $115K. Once a mortgage is paid off on a rental, now you have to make a decision to keep it paid off, or refinance the property and reinvest the money from the refinance into another rental property, dividend stocks, or reinvest in your business. My opinion is to pay off around half the properties. If you have a total of 10 properties, pay off 4 of them and have one or two with a line of credit and then have 4 with a bank loan (mortgage). Some people don't like to owe money so they will buy a property, pay it off and buy another one and pay off that property as well and repeat the process. If you do decide to refinance the rental, try to stay around 50% or 60% of the value of the rental (LTV = Loan to Value) don't max out your refinance loan. My best friend did this to his rental properties and now every month he barely breaks even on the property and if something breaks or he has a vacancy, he is sweating bullets. So don't max out the refinance and take every single penny, some investors do but I don't recommend it.

Never refinance a property and use that money to go shopping, remodel your kitchen, buy a car, or anything like this. I had a co-worker that bought a four-plex at a great low price, after having the property for about 7 years, she refinanced the property and bought a new car, went shopping, vacation, and bought clothing. Now she is paying interest on that money so she could go shopping. Her expenses have gone up and she has less money every month. Now if something breaks, has a vacancy, or if her insurance goes up in cost on the 4-plex, then these expenses come out of her savings account. At least she can write off the interest on her taxes, but every time one unit is vacant, she loses money at a rental rate of $700 to $800 a month and it is hard to make up for that lost rental income.

Tip:
Here is a tip that can help out your friends that have a mortgage. If you make one extra payment per year of the whole amount of the monthly payment, note with escrow, you will pay off your mortgage in about 16 to 18 years or so, depending on the balance and interest rate. They have plenty of mortgage calculators that can show you the breakdown of how many months you will have left and principle & interest.

For vacancies, when a tenant gives you the notice that they are about to move out, start getting things lined up right away, the listing for the property, the cleaning supplies, paint. Start making arrangements for cleaning services and repairmen to start work on the property right away so you can start showing the house to new clients and this is the key to rental properties. Act fast and get the property listed fast. Sometimes I list a property before the old tenant moved out depending on the permission of the tenant and the condition of the house. If the tenant kept the house clean and organized, then I will make arrangements with the tenant letting them know that every Wednesdays and Saturdays at 5 pm, I will be showing the house to new clients. Sometimes the tenant will agree 100%, sometimes they want to change the days or times which is fine as long as it works for both parties. Try to set a plain appointment, set up the appointments for groups, and don't just set the appointment for one person. If the showing is Saturday at 5 pm, then tell everybody to show up on Saturday at 5 pm. Trust me you will have many cancellations and you would have wasted hours. Plus this will show urgency to the other tenants that they are not the only ones interested and that the tenant has competition for the house.

I had one house with a vacancy and three families showed up all at once and the last family loved the house and wanted it right away so they stayed longer to talk and as we were talking another family showed up to see the house and they liked it as well, and needless to say they wanted it right away and I emailed them the application and the very next day they had the application, employment info, proof of income and the deposit and the 1st month's rent in cash. They lived in the house for two years and when they were ready to move out, the sister and grandmother wanted to move in right away. Didn't even have to show the property and had no vacancy, it was a smooth transition. Don't forget to always get the deposit and 1st month's rent in cash, if not you will get a canceled check or a bounced check. If they can't get the cash, ask them to borrow it from friends, coworkers, or family members. Let the family be the bank and worry about the deposit.

This is a good process to do, one time I had a person that gave me the deposit and 1st month's rent and two weeks later I get a phone call saying they changed their minds and they wanted to move to another state, I explained to them over the phone and said "I am sorry to hear you are moving, but you know this is nonrefundable." She said I know but a job opportunity came up and I am moving and the company is paying for everything. This is why it's a good thing I received cash because I bet I would have received a canceled check or NSF notice in the mail. Charge extra if they are going to let other adults live in the house, like an Aunt, Uncle, or a friend. Let them know in the beginning when signing the lease that the lease agreement is between person "name" and/or person "name," charge an extra fee for other adults. Trust me they are charging them rent to live in your property. Don't let them paint the rooms unless they give you the cash to paint it back, if not you will be stuck with a paint color like pink or purple that no one likes. When going over the lease agreement, take down their driver's license information and check the stubs for their place of employment.

Get enough rentals that you can handle, maybe 6 to 12. Whatever you can keep up with for as long as you can, till you have to get someone to help run the properties for you. Which leads to another expense, some property management companies want 10% of the rent and 60% of the first month's rent to manage the property and to find a tenant for the lease agreement. If two real estate agents are involved in finding a tenant for the house, it's a total of a 60% fee of the 1st month's lease and 30% goes to the agent representing the tenant and 30% to the listing agent that listed it on MLS.

Don't invest just in one neighborhood, get to know your clientele and area. Keep the rentals diverse, if some of your tenants work at the same factory, then get rentals in another area of the town as well. What will happen if that factory closes? Then you are left with a bunch of rental properties that you might have a hard time renting out.

Here are some numbers that can give you an idea of how things could be with rentals, now some numbers will change by location, type of house, economy, and condition of the house.

One of your goals with rentals is to get 1% of the value of the house as rent or more if possible. For example, if the house is worth $120,000 X 1% = $1,200 a month in rent. *Expenses = (insurance, taxes, repairs, mortgage)*

House 1 - Rent = $1,200 – expenses = $550 gross profit per month
House 2 - Rent = $1,100 – expenses = $425 gross profit per month
House 3 - Rent = $1,200 – expenses = $475 gross profit per month

This is only three properties making $1,450 a month in gross profit, now this can help pay some bills, imagine if you had 5 or 10 houses.

Each property is going to have a different mortgage, insurance rate, and interest rate. The repairs will vary. (Results will vary as well)

Keep in mind that Real Estate can be risky as well so that is why it's not always a great idea to put all your investments into real estate. Section 8 changes the calculations of how much it will pay out. Because of the issue of accidents on the property (make sure you get liability insurance), the federal government changed the rules and guidelines on flood insurance and now you have a higher policy rate for rental properties. Neighborhoods can witness an increase in crime and good families and tenants may start moving out because the neighborhood is bad, so keep an eye on the neighborhood.

If you are not interested in investing in real estate by yourself or you hate the idea of dealing with tenants and making repairs. You do have another option that is available and they are called joint ventures, were you and a few other investors invest in a specific property for a set minimum amount ranging from $50K to $100K depending on what the property is and the minimum to invest.

Example of numbers

You have the minimum amount to invest $50,000 and the property cost $200,000 for a 4-plex then your ownership is 25% so your profit per month is 25%

Rent per unit is $800 per month so the total rent will be $3200
Minus property management fees (usually 10% to 15%) = $320
Minus insurance and taxes = $900

Minus any repairs per month Avg. = $300
Minus Vacancy depending on area = $80
Profit per month is $1600 * 25% = $400 per month
So now your $50K investment makes you $400 per month $4,800 per year for a 9.6% return just by investing.

If interested in this option in the New Orleans area, then email me at jason@webuyrentsell.com for more info on investing with groups and let someone else deal with the headaches. Also, another great thing is that you can spread out your investments easily. Check out your local real estate club to see if they have any opportunities to do a group investment.

Just like a resume, you need to keep up with your financial statements. This is like your resume for banks, keep your financial statements up to date every year. At first, I hated doing this, but once I got the hang of it and made an excel file from one of the bank forms, it became a lot easier. This will help when you are comparing with a friend or another real estate investor, nothing wrong with a little competition. You actually need this for your bank loans, so this file will make the process so much easier.

On the next tab of the excel file, save the info of each rental property like taxes, insurance, date of purchase, air filter, the size of the house, lot size and gas or electric. This info is great especially when you have to re-list the property and show this info to a bank.

Tip:
The deal of a lifetime happens every month, there is always another great deal. Just be patient and keep looking.

Don't forget they have a few other ways to make money in the Real Estate market, buy, fix and flip, wholesaling, tax liens and other liens, apartments, REITS, commercial properties and a few others. This is another reason why I like real estate so much because you have many options available.

Real Estate Success Story

After Hurricane Katrina hit New Orleans, everything was ruined and devastated throughout the area. I knew an investor that had 3 duplexes in Chalmette, LA that was flooded and had to be gutted out and rebuilt. The owner of the duplexes didn't give up, he didn't throw in the towel, he did what he had to do to fix them and be back in business. So he got started right away before he even got a check from the insurance company. As he was half-way through after a few months, people were coming by to ask if they can live there and if they can fill out an application. The owner was a little bit shocked that people were coming around to ask if they can live there. Some of the other homes in the area did not even start gutting out the house and nothing had been done. He also started receiving some checks in the mail from the insurance company to rebuild the rentals. A few months later, the owner of a few duplexes from four street away came by and wanted to talk to the owner about how he was done with rentals and he gutted the houses and was just going to sell and retire. So he made a deal to sell him the three houses for the value of the land and $0.10 on the dollar for the structure. Plus this investor was a handy man and he knew how to do a lot of work himself and he knew a lot of people that were contractors. So he was able to save a lot of money on the work and rent the duplexes in no time and he had the other duplexes rebuilt and rented in no time as well. He owns all 6 duplexes free in clear in a couple of years, retired at the age of 33 and all he does is be with his family, travel, and manage his investment properties.

When dealing with repairs on rentals, nothing is cheap. Almost everything is between $150 to $200 bucks on the cheap side and depending on the job, it can be $1,000 to $2000. If you have the option of learning how to carry out some of these repairs, you can save so much money. If you can learn how to be a plumber, it will pay off big time. When you know how to replace a hot water heater or repair a toilet, you can save $250 bucks. Don't be scared to try, if you are not successful, then you can always say well at least I tried, let me call someone. Some people refuse to try or give it a shot and they say "I don't know anything about it." When they ask the repairman what he did, they get shocked that the repairman gets the job done in 20 minutes and they are like "that was fast," here is your bill of $125 for the repairs."

Before I quit my job, I knew I needed a stable income, so I invested in rental properties at first then REITS (Real Estate Investment Trusts) and other dividend paying stocks, till I got to a point where it was too much between my job and managing my properties. I knew I needed to take it to the next level with my investment plan and diversify. So I started a business on the side while holding my job and rentals which was difficult. An e-commerce site for selling products online that I made in my garage. Whenever I received an order, I will go to the garage, make the product, then pack and ship it.

Real Estate Helpful Websites

www.Realtor.com
www.Homepath.com
www.hudhouses.com
www.HudHomeStore.com
www.Postlet.com is now www.Zillow.com
www.jasonballay.com/realestate
www.auction.com

Books I found Helpful

"Rich Dad Poor Dad" by Robert Kiyosaki
"Millionaire Real Estate Investor" by Gary Keller
"Real Estate Day Trading" by Larry Goins

5TH CHAPTER BUSINESS
Investment Plan Section: Business & Other Types of Income

The very first business venture I did was with my brother. Then, I was 17 and my brother was 20, we bought into a distributor agreement to sell home decor items. We bought a website, sent out catalogs, showed the items to some friends and family, and we didn't get any sales, not one. Guess who was the best customer? Me, I was their best customer and I thought the items were so cool and I still have these items till this day. Also, my brother started a new job working long hours and he started to put the business to the side because he had no time because he was exhausted from work and I was left running the business by myself. So after a few months, I cut my losses and moved on because I couldn't run it by myself and then split the profits, if we had any sales to an absent partner.

The business I started is something that worked for me and I was happy doing it. But not something that might work for you. So this is something for you to decide. One of the problems I had was trying to duplicate what the next guru was doing and I was thinking; hey if he can sell this item, then I can sell it too. With no luck I repeated this process over and over again, chasing the next big money-making idea with no results. The only person that was making the money was the person selling the next big idea that can make you rich. Then I learned you have to be unique, some kind of advantage over the competition. Also, you need to educate yourself with money and investments.

Once I got to a comfortable level with my rentals and

dividend stocks, I wanted to take it to the next level. So I started looking into an online business selling products that were made in my garage. I didn't want to leave my comfort zone yet so I went to the company I worked for and asked for a raise with the goal I had in mind which was a 20% increase. They denied it saying that the company works on tight margins and they did a lot of investments back into the business and the list of reason went on and on. So I turned to plan B, I took the resume I had updated every year and started to send it out to other companies. It took 4 to 5 months but I was able to get something that was paying 40% increase and the key to this is to reinvest these new higher paychecks and not start spending away. Good thing I left because while I was still there, the company was in defense mode and was checking to see if I was doing something wrong, and giving me more work so they could replace me because I asked for that raise.

Good thing I did reinvest my extra income because the retailer got bought out and they cut us a lump sum and guess what I did with that check? You guessed it, all I did was reinvest it into some dividend stocks and I bought another piece of equipment to take my business to the next level to offer another service.

If you decide to start a business, this will help also with dividend portfolio because you will have a better understanding of how business works from the beginning to end process.

Look into investing in a franchise and with your building assets, you will be able to get a franchise approval and loan.

Pros: they have a process in place and usually a great marketing plan. Easier to get loans because a bank will see you having a better chance of being successful.
Some of the cons with a real good franchise are; they usually have a nice price tag to go with it and you need a

large down payment. Some franchises will help you out with this on how to get the money and where to go for the loans. You have to follow their process, look, guidelines, and you can't do something outside of their policies.

Great feeling to have to work to invest in yourself and your investment house.

Financial Freedom

After a period of time, plan B (investment plan) will just be no more plan B but a lifestyle and plan B will be plan A and you will notice a change in your view about money. You will feel better that you have a backup income even as you develop multiple streams of income. The wealthy has this mindset of how they can create multiple streams of income. The wealthy don't rely on just one source of income.

Business Helpful Websites

www.sba.gov
www.entrepreneur.com

Books I found Helpful

"Rich Dad Poor Dad" by Robert Kiyosaki
The E-Myth Revisited by Michael E. Gerber
Incorporate & Grow Rich! By Allen; Hill; Kennedy
"Get Rich Click!" by Marc Ostrofsky
"The Millionaire Real Estate Agent" by Gary Keller – I know it's
real estate by it's a great book for the business mindset.

Other types of Income

Blog Ads

Get paid to write a blog, when people click on your ad in your blog, you get a certain amount of money per click depending on the ad and competitiveness of the topic. I remember the first check I received in the mail, it was around $108 dollars. It took over 6 months but it was free money that I reinvested.

Tip:
I noticed people that made money on the internet had many websites and they did not just have one website. Plus if you are going to get the knowledge and know-how of how to run a website, then you should use the knowledge on building other sites as well.

YouTube Ads

At this time (2015) I don't have a YouTube money making account but I heard of a few people that don't have to work anymore because they get so much from ads, views, and great content that YouTube sends them a check. This is something to look into and get some details.

Affiliate Programs aka JV Partners

Is great if you have a blog or website, companies will cut you a check if the customer buys their product or service and you get a percentage of the sales. I still do this and I still get a few hundred dollar checks. I even offer an Affiliate program for my websites. BeerShirts.co have a program where the Blogger or website owner gets a promo code and every time someone uses their code or link, the customer gets a discount on their order and the Affiliate gets a commission in the mail. They have many Affiliate programs out there to choose from and you will not have any problems finding some. I was an Affiliate with a Lending Company when I use to do mortgages and I use to get a few checks in the mail. Also if you own a website or plan on building an online business, then get an Affiliate program too. Don't be like me and think I can get my own customers, usually, these affiliates have access to over 10K to 100 thousand clients, and followers– plus this is a great way to grow your sales force without the labor and you only pay when you get a sale.

Selling Products Online

Do you like making things with your hands? You can sell your homemade objects on Etsy.com and Artfire.com (plus a few others) they offer a complete shopping cart system to list items and process transactions. They also have a huge following of customers that like to shop on their site. If you don't want to make things, just want to sell products, you can sign up with a shopping cart host that can process your orders, like Shopify.com and Bigcommerce.com. Before doing this, make sure you are selling items that are unique and not a program where everyone has access to the items.

EBooks/Digital files

If you can teach someone on a subject or you have info that can help with their lives, this is a great option. I became interested in this when I saw some friends at a birthday party or someone at the gym and they asked me what I did for a living. I told them what I did and they were interested and wanted to know more and they told me they would love to do that stuff. What should we invest in? Should I do real estate? What is it like and how do we get started and then a conversation would be for hours and I knew I only scratched the surface of the information and at the end of the conversation my friends said you should be a teacher and show people how to do this and that you do a great job of explaining subjects. So now I tell people to check out my blog and if they wanted more info, they can buy my eBooks. Do you have information to share and think people will pay for or a great story to tell and a great creative mind? Then this can be a great option to look into. Check out Clickbank.com / GumRoad.com on where to sell digital media.

Read this book for more information on internet income "Get Rich Click!" by Marc Ostrofsky lots of useful information and this was the book that caught my attention. He said you are an author/teacher first, then you are an investor, marketer, or whatever you do to make your money.

Business Partnerships

Later on when you are fully developed, you might want to step out of the box and start investing in others and start lending a hand to help to grow someone's business as a partnership so you can increase your return. Like the investors you see on TV and those that invest in business owners and work to build a better company.

Buying a Business

This can be a great way to get into the business world. There are many advantages of buying an existing business. Usually, the business has a system already in place, all the licenses are in place and most importantly established a customer base. They do have some cons like, if the business is for sale, then why are they selling, what are the reasons behind it? A perfect example is; I found a Daiquiri and Bar Business up for sale, I met with the business broker, talked on the phone about the business many times, went to the business location a few times and everything seem to be good and everything was adding up.

The reason why they were selling was because they

owned a restaurant and could not manage both locations at once. I found out that they were really food people and the bar was something they bought as a combo deal. I was excited and was about to sign the papers and give them the deposit check but that night I asked someone else to go there and tell me what they think about the place and if they like it. The morning I was about to sign, I checked my phone after getting dressed and had two missed phone calls and a voice mail. I listened to the voice mail and nothing good was reported from that night, I called my friend and he gave me the details of what was wrong and what he didn't like about the business.

I called the business broker and canceled the meeting and told him I was not interested. So be cautious and just keep digging into the business before you sign the papers and hand over a deposit check. I know of people that have bought businesses before and they become good deals and are very happy. If you decide to invest in a franchise, most of all franchise require assets and a down payment, they can offer in-house financing to pay for the rest. Since you are investing in real estate and/or dividend stocks, an asset portfolio becomes a lot easier to achieve a franchise approval. Remember you have to follow their rules and their policies and procedures.

For so many ideas to make some side money and start a small business check out these 101 Business ideas, I am sure you will find something that will catch your attention: www.entrepreneur.com/article/283723

Marketing- Let's talk about Marketing.
...marketing is the task of getting people to call and blow up your phone.

Apart from people asking me how I got into real estate and investing in stocks. They would also ask me what I did for a living, and I will tell people I have a website and I sell products online. Then they will ask me all kinds of questions like how do you rank number 1 on Google and how do you manage your social media? How do you do online marketing, what can I do with AdWords? How do I get traffic, and the list goes on and on. I was at a networking event where they would have guest speakers talk about business and I would go to these events like chamber of commerce, Fuel Nola (local business network), and people would ask me these same questions on how do you do all this online stuff where do I begin and I will give them advice and explain the process out to them and I will give them my number if they had any questions. Months later, one of the members called me and left a voice mail and said who he was that we met at the Fuel Nola event and that he was looking for help with his website.

I called him back and he asked about being ranked number one on Google and wanted to meet me. So we talked for an hour and I explained to him the process and he said "Jason I appreciate your knowledge and your help but I sell cars and that's it, I don't know anything about what you just said, can you do this for me and I will pay you to do it?" I was so shocked that he asked me to do this for him, I was only doing this for a few years, and I didn't want to screw up. Without even thinking of a price I said sure not a problem, I can start tonight and get the process started he said "great thank you very much" I worked for him for a few days a week with SEO (search engine optimization) and some social media marketing and advice and after a few weeks, I was done and I told him "you should be all set" and gave him a list of things to do in the future.

The car salesman said "how much do I owe you" I said let's make it an even $500 bucks. He smiled and said "you are too kind" and he cut me a check for $1000 and said, "you have no idea how much we were paying people in New York to do what you just did and the bad answers we use to get from them." He said "you should do this for a living," I smiled and laughed a little bit and I said "really, you think I could do just this for a living?" and he said "absolutely!" I didn't think nothing of it and just stayed focus on my investments and working on online business and then my friend asked me "Jason do you know anyone that does SEO?" I have a lot more competitors in my area and I want to be number one on everything. I replied him and I said yeah I know someone that does SEO and he said: "who?" I replied "me," but you don't have to pay someone to do this, you can do it and we talked for an hour about suggestions, customer reviews, marketing, and standing out from the rest. So after a few months, he said: "Jason can I pay you to help me out with this?" He said I am too busy running my business and don't have the time to deal with it. I said yeah I can do this for you but at that time, I had no clue how much to charge but I think I am onto something here. I love marketing and I like helping people to hit their goals and make their money. After that, I started pursuing online marketing. So those of you going into online business or in need of help with your local social media marketing, let me know if you need help and I and my team will assist you with your goals and marketing needs.

If interested in our marketing services let us know at
www.nvumarketing.com
jason@nvumarketing.com

We offer services for SEO, Social Media, Email Marketing, Internet Traffic, Web Design and Hosting, Tee Shirts with Company Logo, Business Cards, and more services to come.

Another thing I want to add at this point is; look at this situation, I started off with this one little business and then a better opportunity came along for a better business. So it just goes to show that you never know what other opportunities are around the corner. My little online business gave me the knowledge and know-how of how things work in the online world.

Notes:

6TH CHAPTER
Book Recap Notes/Tips

So after reading this book, your investment plan should be something like this, with work, side jobs, online sales, business, real estate and any other money making activity on top, investing in dividend paying stocks, or if you chose to focus on real estate only, then under **Investments** change it to Real Estate instead of Dividend Stocks, the choice is yours. After some years, you will focus all your time and energy on real estate and other times you will focus on dividend stocks. As for me, I find myself focusing on Real Estate. Just remember to let your investments pay the bills, food, housing and other expenses. If you have to work for money or you are going to receive that money once, then reinvest that money.

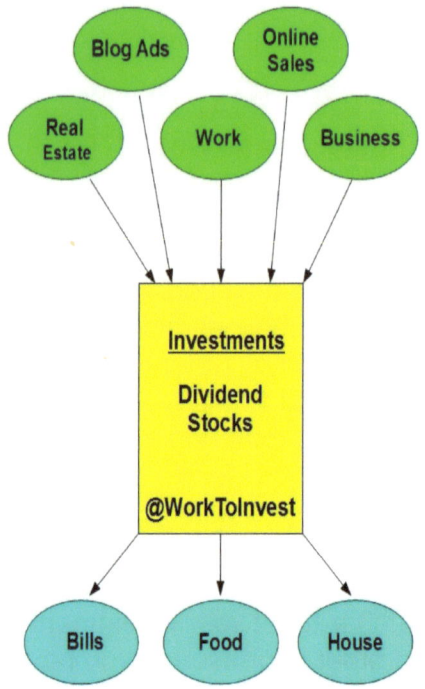

Just remember investing is for the long-term, it's not something that is going to make you a millionaire. It's not going to happen overnight, two years, or even 5 years, it's a process, a lifestyle change and something that needs to be passed on to generations. It's what you put into it, if you only put 10% into it, then you will see 10% results if you put only a few hours into it, then you will only see a few hours worth of work. I hear people all the time say, I will put 6% or 10% the maximum amount of my salary into my 401k and spend the rest, I tell them the hell with that, save like you are about to lose your job, invest as much as you can. It's more likely you are going to have a lot saved up and invested and hopefully if done correctly, you will be able to make money from it every month. I read an article about people who retired with a million dollars in their 401K. When I saw this, I was like okay this person retired with a 401K, let me see what they said and after reading, it took the person 32 years to retire. That's why I am not a big fan of 401K, these programs were made for the poor, not for the rich. The people managing the 401k (fund managers) are the ones getting rich FYI. I just heard on the radio how professors are suing the university because the fund managers charge high fees and that the university didn't negotiate a better rate and now these professors have less money to retire with and all those years of hard work to build up their 401K short changed.

Start taking care of your health and body to live a long life by working out, exercising and engaging in activities that are fun like skiing, tennis, basketball and swimming. But remember to do it and have a schedule doing and eating right and healthy. Stay away from processed foods and have a high alkaline diet, foods high in alkaline like almonds, grapes, banana, apple, berries, orange, broccoli, lettuce, cucumber, peas, and so many other items. Remember you are in this for the long haul so live a healthy life, set your mind to live long, think of living a long life.

Surround yourself with family and good friends. Try to surround yourself with people that are positive minded and a great influence on your life. Someone that will bring you up and motivate you. If someone is bringing you down, then they need to hang out with someone else that is similar to them. Teach your loved ones and children this process, keep the investment house growing and explain to your kids the importance of investing and to pass down their investments to their kids.

Tip:
Here is a fun tip, when setting up passwords and if you have to use a symbol use the money sign "$" By adding this to passwords, it will help remind you to reinvest your funds, this was a tip from another investor.

Always keep learning and teaching yourself, start buying

books in specific fields to get a greater knowledge of the industry. Keep expanding your knowledge, never stop learning. I am a big fan of audio books, I don't listen to the radio or news a lot. I keep going through my audio books, there is nothing wrong with getting knowledge while sitting in traffic and driving to work.

Set your goal at $10 million in assets not just $1 million in assets, hell you can hit this goal with 8 houses on average – think big, I encourage you to go for more than a million. There is no shortage of money, the only shortage we have is people thinking big.

I grew up poor, my mother was working two jobs to raise a family of 4, I was unemployed for almost a year, and I joined the mortgage business at the worst time, 6 months before the housing crash, after that unemployed again, so I know what it's like not to have money... like Bill Gates said, *"If you're born poor, it's not your mistake. But if you die poor, it is your mistake."* – I invest everything twice a year so I am poor twice out of that year and let my money do the work for me.

Avoid debt that doesn't pay you – Make it a rule that you never use debt that won't make you money. I borrowed money for a car only because I knew it could increase my income when delivering products and hauling equipment and tools. Investors use debt to leverage investments and grow cash flows. Poor people use debt to buy things that make rich people richer.

I like these little saying:

"Save to invest, don't Save to Save, the only reason to save money is

to invest it."

...Put your saved money into a secured, sacred (untouchable) accounts. Never use these accounts for anything, not even an emergency.

...It's not what I do, it's what I do with my income that matters

Social Websites follow us, and please share:

Website:
www.worktoinvest.com

Blog:
www.jasonballay.com

Facebook:
https://www.facebook.com/pages/Plan-B-for-Income/1643503915902971

Twitter:
https://twitter.com/worktoinvest
@worktoinvest

Google+

Instagram:
@worktoinvest

Need more help?
Interested in a one on one training session or Webinars
Email me: jason@worktoinvest.com

W2I CRUISE

I always like helping people to achieve their goals, I like meeting other people with the same goals to help them to grow their investments and business. Whenever I know that two people would benefit each other and they can both grow their business. I would do my best to get these two individuals together. One of my goals in the future is to have some kind of mastermind group on a cruise ship, or a special location, to have a guest speaker and meeting with like minded people to talk about what is going on in the industry. To get people to help other people and to exchange ideas. Plus what's wrong with having a cruise and a business trip at the same time. For comments on this, send me an email: jason@worktoinvest.com

Disclosure

This information is provided to you as a resource for informational purposes only. It is being presented without consideration of the investment objectives, risk tolerance or financial circumstances of any specific investors and might not be suitable for all investors. Past performance is not indicative of future results. Investing involves risk including the possible loss of principal. This information is not intended to, and should not, form a primary basis for any investment decision that you may make. Always consult your own legal, tax or investment advisor before making any investment, tax, estate and financial planning considerations or decisions.

ABOUT THE AUTHOR
JASON BALLAY

Jason Ballay is a real estate investor, dividend investor, and entrepreneur. His passion for helping people to increase their income and to create multiple streams of income with a great feeling. He loves helping people to get out the rat race and stop living pay check to pay check. Just remember work to invest not work to pay bills. Thank You!